# The Secret Thoughts
## Prose and Poems

Volume One

# The Secret Thoughts
## Prose and Poems

Volume One

Pam Ng Ig Ok

ATHENA PRESS
LONDON

The Secret Thoughts
Prose and Poems


ISBN 10-digit: 1 84748 173 6
ISBN 13-digit: 978 1 84748 173 3

First Published 2008 by
ATHENA PRESS
Queen's House, 2 Holly Road
Twickenham TW1 4EG
United Kingdom

Printed for Athena Press

*For Charlene and Cassidy*
*Two different kinds*

*Apart from the pieces clearly dedicated to specific people, the author asserts: 'It is mere coincidence if you see yourself in any of the pieces.'*

# *Acknowledgements*

Thanks to Rev C Smith (Lady), who suggested that I put my thoughts in writing.

Thanks to Rev Jonathan Hopcroft, who read initial pieces. When he stopped laughing, he suggested that I send them off to publishers for appraisal. He placed the pieces at the altar of Chelmsford Cathedral and said a little prayer. How amazing.

Appreciation to Martin Lawford and Irene Sampson: admin, Peggy Potter: healing hands, Jane Walters: bell-ringer, and Kathy Stone for being there.

My father, Sir Nicholas, stood by me whilst words came pouring out. May he rest in perfect peace.

*Contents*

# Part One
# Self-Determination

*Contents*

## *Sadness and Solitude*

One feels so sad and lonely today,
More than ever before,
Intense the desire to escape,
Total depression looms,
Consequently total darkness.

Wallow not in self-pity;
Get into this, get into that,
Get into everything you could.
So preoccupied. So overwhelmed.
To notice the forlorn state of affairs.

One feels so sad and lonely today,
More than ever before.
Don't push it;
A little nudge will hasten the
Fall into the gloom of darkness.

She wallowed not in self-pity,
Has been into this,
Has been into that,
Has been into everything she could;
Yet sadness and loneliness persist.

## *Niche*

Whilst climbing out of the abyss I found my unrelenting niche;
Solving a scattered and chaotic jigsaw puzzle,
Rather indescribable,
I promise to try.

You are worth zilch.
You are nobody.
A vacuous waste of space,
Better off dead and buried.

'Who are you? Who are you?'
He constantly queried.
*Who am I? Who am I?*
I constantly pondered.

The arduous task in self-determination began,
I persevered fervently and nothing else mattered.
In the end I found myself in a deep ravine;
I fell into the hole ages ago without comprehension.

What a jigsaw puzzle,
Totally scattered and chaotic.
I gathered the pieces and proceeded to assemble the lot;
Two-piece a fortnight I can manage a pace.

I have eternity to suture bit by bit,
I'd toil till every piece is slotted back into place.
I finally found my niche,
Rebuilding my broken and scattered life.

## *Head in the Miasma*

My head in the miasma,
Everything so billowy, cloudy and hazy.
Had I consumed the picked wild mushrooms
An answer may be found.
Had I kissed the leapt pond toads 'n' newts
An answer may be found.

All so dimly and vaguely
The white talc strewn around.
Whilst I have my head in the miasma,
Might as well head to Miami.
Miami, here I come to thee at last.
My head buried in the miasma!

## *Limbo*

Hanging here in limbo waiting for Armageddon,
No place to call my humble abode,
Rooted in this familiar environment,
Far away from home, so lost.
Entire being refused to adapt.
Home is where the heart is, the adage
Preyed on my mind incessantly.

Years on I toured in search of humble home.
Familiar succours seemed to have vanished;
Landmarks dissipated and fallen away,
Aghast in awesome wonder,
Where is the home I used to know?
No place to call my humble abode.

Back again to my acquired abode,
An empty shelf stands in its place.
No longer the familiar environment,
No more urge to ingrate.
Lost my root and foundation,
No place to call my humble home,
Hanging here in limbo waiting for Armageddon.

## *B4 I Bow Out*

Just before the grand finale,
I must get down from my pinnacle.
I must admit that I have been beat;
Overwhelmed with weariness and fatigue.
I must admit that I have been beat;
I seek no more approval or appreciation,
Have no more zeal to give satisfaction.
Time has come to say goodbye,
Seeing that I am exhausted
I must depart in
Peace.

## *Jinx*

Oh baby, you are jinxed,
You are reliving the ancient curse yet again.
Search yourself;
Whatever the matter?
Shouldn't have prayed in that temple in Makeros Avenue Kibrus;
Shouldn't have kissed those effigies and statues;
Shouldn't have promised to love him for ever in blood;
Shouldn't have promised the gods your heart.
Time and time again you had the dream,
Hoping to wake up but all in vain.
You are already awake but
Hapless 'n' jinxed.

## *Hot Pursuit*

Forever in hot pursuit of what you can't get,
If it is meant to be, it is all yours already.
Pursuing what's not yours does nothing but wears
  you out,
Lassitude and weariness lead to disillusionment.
Save yourself the angst and torment;
Commence a hot pursuit for what you can get.
Aim for the sky,
Stretch your hands as far as you can reach,
Grab whatever is given to you.
Voila! Presto!
Unwind and relax,
It's all yours to keep.

## *ESP*

Consult your innermost sense,
Messages await immediate attention.
Forgotten the password?
You know yourself the best,
Jog your memory.
Await a pop-up.
Not able to logon still?
Pay heed to your intuition,
The hunch. The sixth sense.
The subtle but essential password.
The ESP.

## *Providence*

My fate, my destiny,
All but a singleton.
In constant battle,
One is petrified.

Not in physical brawl
Lest you think crazy head.
Constant searching of body and soul,
Quest for the other half of me.

All alone but ready to go,
Besieged by simpletons,
The déjà vu sensation
Spooks and freaks me out.

Relationship so far-fetched,
Yet to master the elusive game.
Intimacy a fanciful urge,
Despite recurring celestial hints.

History repeats itself.
One is destined unlucky in love.
Do adhere to the celestial hints.
One is destined to be alone.

## *Hall Mirror*

I looked into the hall mirror
Late last night,
Saw myself the very first time.
Almost transparent and pallid,
Ashen form peered right back at me.
The reflection distorted and awry,
Manifestation of the life gone wrong.

'Come hither, madam,' the reflection beckoned,
'Wither thou you shrivel and die,
Wither thou you fade and wilt.
You fade and wilt. You shrivel and die.'
I looked into the hall mirror
Late last night,
Saw myself the very last time.

## *No More Tears*

No more tears.
Parched ducts arid dry,
Burnt ochre eyes aglow.
Unshed tears.
No more streaming water drops,
Anguished throbbing heart aches;
No more teardrops,
The soothing fluid.

No more tears.
Not lubricated, no runny fluid,
Burnt amber eyes aglow.
Unshed tears.
Crushed throbbing heart aches;
Poignant grief lacerates tender heart.
No more safeguarding,
Let the living water flow.

## *Motherhood*

Engulfed with foreboding,
Motherhood,
Ill-prepared, ill-primed.
Seed sown,
Ready to erupt;
Not ready,
Pregnant damsel.

Awed sense of responsibility,
Motherhood,
Ill-timed, ill-prepared.
Entrusted bundle,
Growth of life;
Not ready,
Mother and child.

Progressive and challenging,
Motherhood,
Awed sense of responsibility.
All at stake,
All agog,
Ready or not,
Women who dare.

## *On the Verge*

The big picture perched on the wall,
Exposed to the elements.
Caught between two enemy-fires driven to ruination,
In cahoots negotiating rain and sun.

Zillion cracks, the brainchild of ultraviolet rays.
Pelts of acid rain through the zillion cracks.
Botched up vision
Reminiscent of both elements.

Variegated hue, the blanched face,
Wrinkled in tiny nought and crosses draft.
Scrawny hands, scraggy spider crabs,
Sunken eyes deep set in eerie ghostly sockets.

The big picture perched on a thin thread,
Not a pretty one to display.
Stay the urge to dismount and leave,
The dismantling urge to stay and live.

## *The Cock and the Hen*

The cockerel flew off the handle,
Bobbing its tiny head at the hen.
Flapping its wing nondescriptly,
Squawking and cuckooing its intention.

The hen flew off the ledge,
Scratching through with claws on spindle legs.
Mollycoddling and cosseting the chicks,
Squawking and declining the cock's intent.

The hen: the cock;
Allegory man and wife,
Symbolism you and I,
Squabbling and mirroring the same effect.

## *Chugging Wheel*

Chugging wheel,
Bespoke spokes.
Held together by the golden knob,
Slowly up the slippery hill,
Rapidly down the cobbled lane,
Chug and tug,
Pull and hold,
Held together by the golden knob.

Chugging wheel,
Bespoke folks.
Held together by the burning urge,
Slowly up the righteous path,
Rapidly down the damning ditch,
Scorn and sneer,
Deride and mock,
Held together by the burning urge.

## *Zing the Bell*

Deep-rooted attraction
Embedded in far-reaching fear of death
Fanatically attached to the big bell.
My gigantic dormant bell.

Ever so close by my bed
Ready to toll if I despair,
Should the grim reaper reappear,
A chiming bell. A pealing bell.

Twice the rhyming, chiming bells,
Twice the great grim escape.
Two decades apart,
So fresh in mind.

Consolation with the bell in view,
My head is laid to rest at night.
Dormant bell at length at work,
Should I ever again despair.

## *Almost There!*

If I could understand the answers,
They could teach me the questions.
It matters not what you ask and how,
The answers fit when the questions are right.
Even in destitution an exit exists,
To and fro the abyss of Waltham Abbey.
Either in departure or in arrival
Through the gaping orifice.
I cast my mind to the choices;
If I could understand the questions,
The answers could be easier than presumed.
A step in time towards the exit,
Almost there!
If I have the right questions to answer.

## *Obtuse Angels*

Mired in deep depression,
Full of churlish suggestions.
She ran into St John, Peter and Paul,
Innards, body and soul.
Expecting angelic intervention,
She emptied her soul.
Albatross, the bane of her life, flew around in rage.
Checked by the virtuous angels,
Obtuse, the abysmal ones intervened.
Object of calumny, tittle-tattle and tale.
Innards, body and soul.
Shackled in greater bondage,
She ran back out in chains,
Mired in deeper depression.

*Obtuse Angels (sketch by Stephen Parkinson)*

## *Million Dreams*

Deep within me,
A thousand emotions,
Lukewarm warmth,
Burning desire to arrive;
Destination still unknown.
In the still of the night,
Trekking through Twankhams alley,
Trudging fundamentally in search,
A thousand times and counting.
Moonlight shadows hanging loosely by,
Free spirit, invisible touch of love.
Whether the weather be good or bad,
Prowling through, holding on to hope,
Eppingen, Essex, town of million dreams.

*Million Dreams (sketch by Stephen Parkinson)*

## *Open Cans of Worms*

There are cans of worms,
There are more cans of worms,
More cans than ever imaginable.
Cankerworms that gnaw the fabric of our very existence.

Open cans of worms,
Sealed cans of worms,
More cans than ever imaginable.
On tenterhooks, hopeful that sealed cans reflect our very existence.

Open-ended cans of worms,
Sickening, tangled, squirming mesh,
More slippery worms than ever imaginable.
Angst-ridden, on reflection open cans reflect our very existence.

## *My Third Eye*

Watching eye,
My third eye,
In situ prominent on my temple,
Right between my two eyes in situ,
Sees all, wholly invisible to others.
Icon of wholesomeness and purity,
Blind to moral turpitude and decadence,
Eternally open to whiteness and probity.

Ocular eye,
Mystical seeable eye,
In situ prominent on my temple,
Vigilant whilst the others sleep.
Shrouded in alchemy and divination,
Embedded in occultism and wizardry,
Medulla oblongata in consuming feverish quest,
Querying the status of my never-blinking third eye.

## *Beyond John O'Groats*

Walk away my anxiety,
Land's End to John O'Groats,
Converged the lands meet 'n' merged as one.
My anxious legs a step in turn,
Walk away my vagaries yet to death.

Sail away my anxiety,
John O'Groats my starting point.
Far beyond that eyes cannot see.
Ship adrift the ebbing sea,
Sail away my anxiety to eternal rest.

Free at last my anxiety,
Beyond John O'Groats, at last at sea.
Stateless expanse the ebbing sea.
Bobbing ship adrift on tide,
Untying reef knots tightly tied.

*Beyond John O'Groats (sketch by Stephen Parkinson)*

## *Caged Pigeon*

Caged pigeon!
Pigeon-holed and de-winged,
Ablaze with cyclic ideas.
Never the chance to float them all,
Never the chance to spread her wings.

Stored ideas!
Ideally stored and wasted,
Ablaze with pigeon-holed ideas.
Never the chance to flaunt them all,
Never the chance to flee the hole.

Sitting duck!
Walloped whilst sitting on her head,
Bludgeoned senseless in mid-flight.
Never the chance to safely sit,
Never the chance to fly ahead.

New ideas!
Unearthed from within her guts,
Ablaze the gusto to regain her wings.
Never the caged pigeon of yesterday,
Never the sitting duck no more!

## *Bandwagon*

Jump on it,
Why don't we all?
Albeit sheepishly we must adhere,
Lean fast to the magnetic pull,
Pull apart and shred to bits,
Snuff the living daylight out of her,
Lest it shine for all to see.

Jump on it,
Why don't we all?
Albeit sheepishly we must progress
The fallacies, whether true or false.
Jump on board the annihilation boat,
Shred the ailing credibility to bits,
Lest our evil hands be exposed.

Jump on it.
We must abide the mission tide,
Albeit sheepishly we must encroach,
Failing which the tide abates,
Discarding ashore our guilty deeds,
The erroneous canards must be fed,
Lest she sues and wins her case.

# Part Two

# De Facto Ex

*Contents*

## *The Wrong End of the Stick, Mr Carlos*

Contrary to your belief,
You were loved
More than you ever know.
So innocent, love unsullied,
Good golly,
Beyond imagination.

Physical pain,
Emotional pain,
The bond ever so close knit.
Felt the surgeon's every slash,
Good golly,
How I loved you.

Awry towards the end;
There was love,
Then animosity.
Transcends any odium,
Good golly,
How I hated you.

Contrary to your belief,
Neither love,
Nor animosity.
Still handsome, my adonis.
Good golly,
How emotionless 'n' numb.

## *Shame*

Shame on you.
My love for you is wasted.
I cook, I clean, I keep the house.
I make, I mend, I keep the bed.
I wash, I spruce, I keep myself.
What do I get in return?
A wandering, unkempt and loveless man.
Shame on you.
My love for you is wasted.

## *Resolution*

I resolved to
Query your humiliating proposals,
Ignore your gormless remarks,
Disregard the hateful anecdotes;
My best resolution yet,
You do not exist at all.

## *Lethargy*

Here he sleeps yet again, akin to blue whale.
Here he snores yet again, akin to jumbo jet.
The truth be known tonight,
Whether asleep or not.
This lacklustre marriage must end tonight,
Whether asleep or not.

Dearest, can you hear me?
Disillusioned life ebbs away to oblivion.
You promised not to sleep at work;
You promised to work overtime at times.
Here we are six months on,
Sleeping our married life to death.

Stop crying lest he stirs awake,
He sleeps on, sniffles regardless.
Disheartened to say the least,
Not getting any, not tonight.
Cynical disenchanted married life,
Over-rated sex in marriage.

Sacré bleu!

## *Empty Void*

Aroused from the deep slumber,
Already gone two years.
An empty void in place,
The illusory bed mound.
Hand stretched but felt the emptiness.

Absolutely gone indeed,
Two women in tow,
Quite devoted to each in turn.
Utterly mortified, I died in humiliation.
Effortlessly, you reached the chosen destination.

Ghostly calm the chosen life;
What nightmarish thing to endure.
Immediately slumped, I drifted away,
Hoping to sleep off the horrible stint,
Still in deep slumber, to arise in self-contentment.

## *De Facto Ex*

Examination looming,
Revision in motion,
The barking commenced simultaneously.
Right behind it stood and barked,
T'is getting hotter as it barked.
The heat so intense it scorched my neck.
In tune with nature's glorious deafness
Swivelled around I searchingly gazed.
Its mouth was moving rapidly;
Foaming from the corners so to speak.

Mind, soul, body and psyche
Debated unproductively for the purpose of its fury.
Dawned on me it eventually did.
Bless its little doggie soul;
It wants its dinner ready and served.
Might as well do supper as the marriage contract demands.
Utterly switched off since the marriage.
Here, hubby, hubby, here's your supper, barking sir!
Revision in motion,
Examination looming.

## *Clanging Chains*

Remembrance day, the bad old days;
A million pieces shudder in shame.
We laughed at the humourless jokes,
Pretended to believe the fabled tales,
Shut our eyes to the seedless affairs.

The long duration of silent periods,
Aloof and gay, the poise, the gait.
Not interested in anyone but you.
We tried in vain to attract your love;
Failed woefully to catch a break.

Eventually you looked back at home;
So late all had gone asleep,
All gone their separate ways.
Irritated, an ogre emerged,
Sought control without success.

Beatings commenced and never stopped,
Clanging chains you were hauled away.
Not to be seen in padlock 'n' keys;
Solemn, remorseful, you reappeared.
Beatings, clanging chains, you were hauled away.

## *Goody Goody*

May be a little presumptuous;
Where is the handsome meek man?
Where is the betrothed caramel sweet?
Sweet Cadbury's goody goody 'n' meeky meeky.

May be a little vacuous;
Where is the humble caramel sweet?
Caramel man, caramel sweet,
All but extinct; sweet love gone sour.

Plausible Cadbury's resuscitation of the caramel sweets,
Impossible the resurrection of extinct dead love.
Bemoan the soured dead sweet love;
Sweet Cadbury's caramel sweets.

## *The Moniker*

The horrible moniker.
An invention whilst irate,
Only meant to hurt and humiliate.
The moniker stuck,
People stare in awesome wonder.
Had she been in the game?

Here are some clarifications.
You know better than you think.
Prostitutes receive money for their services;
The law as it stands in civilised world.
Whilst you were gone someone was there,
An affair makes no one a pro.

The horrible name is here to stay;
Impacts severely on the children and I.
Affectionately you pretend to love,
Sincerely, if you do,
Tell all and sundry the honest truth.
Pro – a nomenclature invented whilst irate.

# Part Three
# Kith and Kin

*Contents*

## *Beyond the Clouds*

When I came upon the hill of hope
There was no one in the vicinity except the birds.
I cried in vain for my father
Whom I could see floating beyond the hills.
He stopped a while and smiled at me.
He waved and then whispered
In a baritone echo-filled voice:

'I am dead and about to fly away;
I'll wait for you beyond the clouds.
Whatever you decide to do from now,
Do not hurry or rush the flight;
I have eternity to pave the way.
When eventually you make the flight,
I'll be waiting beyond the clouds.'

## *Dear Mother*

Humble mother, Susannah O'King,
Respectable and worthy of emulation.
Stuck in unbearable married life,
Under thick and thin you kept at it.

Marriage lasted until death intervened,
Raised your children to follow suit.
Had they followed suit;
A reputable institution the marital union.

No more divorce, no more separation,
No more children born out of wedlock,
No more quests for DNA tests,
No more warring husbands and wives.

Had the children followed suit?
None at all at the last poll.
Sons and daughters lost their married lives
Fighting the infamous Battle of Divorce.

## *Cassis*

How handsome he looks asleep.
Does he actually belong to us?
Oval face, luscious lips, cute little button nose.
Mocha chocolaty colouring,
What a perfect mixture.
He is all mine,
Praise be.

Praise be to whom, you ask,
Praise be to me, I say.
How handsome can one get?
Muscular arms and legs,
Wavy jet-black hair;
An accomplished footballer at ten,
Plays for North Weald Basset, I heard.
He is all mine,
Praise be.

Make no more noise for he stirs awake,
His demeanour comes to mind.
Amiable, kind and truly cares,
He is the apple of his mother's eyes.
What else can one ask in a son?
Hurry up, awake, my pretty son;
Today the world awaits their prince.
He is all ours,
Praise be.

## *Dear Father*

Gone, but for ever here in spirit.
Every thought embedded in you.
Constantly in conversation with your chi;
The message each time, though loud and clear,
Not entirely reassured.
Chiming bells proclaim your safety;
Free spirit requires no helping hand.
Worry not for the departed ones,
The dead not in parity with the living.

Do not be cross, I beg of you;
So many things are left unsaid.
Do not be cross if I invoke your chi,
The living is trapped, both body and soul.
The priests regurgitate the celestial words;
Never too late to visit with you.
Stagnant in this sorrowful rut,
Totally crushed and traumatised,
One more audience, dear father.

## *Kith and Kin*

Where are my kith and kin
This miserable moment in time,
When they are needed the most?
They may answer my call ultimately
When they are no longer needed.
If they answer my call eventually
They may no longer be heard.

Alert my nearest and dearest;
They are needed today at most.
Rich and famous, in time
One may be far removed from them.
One *is* far removed from them in point of fact,
All their demanding calls are answered
Through thick and thin.

## *Back to Your Father's Place, Litterbug*

Must you leave flotsam and jetsam all over the place?
Found them
Stashed away,
Tucked away,
In obscure places.

Must you leave flotsam and jetsam all over the place?
Found them
Upstairs,
Downstairs,
In odd places.

Must you leave flotsam and jetsam all over the place?
Find them
Somewhere else,
Anywhere else,
It is back to your father's place.

## *Adorable Little Monster*

Sleek 'n' slender with olive skin,
Her smiles and laughter captivate.
Teeth as white as snowflakes;
The very shape of the heart, her lips;
Two vertical upright pillars, her legs;
Gait and steps like a grazing gazelle;
Head of thick hair crowing the oval face;
Sparkling eyes flash at you in anger;
Wakes you up from the dreamy state.

Diabolical to say the least;
Impertinent, she heeds not anything you say.
Overflowing with teenage adrenaline and hormone,
She pounces about with brazen rudeness,
Full of indefinable angst and fury.
One moment sweet and adorable,
Next overcome with fit and tantrum.
Anything on the way smashed and trampled;
Wee brother cowering in his room in fear.

Emphatic and sympathetic;
All have been through the raging phase.
Some more monstrous than others at worst.
During each intermission when peaceful and calm
On reflection she is never sure of the anger source.
I pray that after this rampaging period,
After the teenage hormone has been and gone,
My adorable daughter will emerge and come to light
More adorable than ever before.

## *Back and Forth*

Upheaval and cataclysm
Befit description of modern family institution.
Back and forth, to and fro my father's house;
Back and forth, to and fro my mother's house.
Children never settling in one place,
Helter-skelter, hither, thither;
Forever wondering where to call their home.
To and fro, back and forth.

Never the family spirit of days gone by;
Never the community spirit of family life.
None settling and chaotic;
Fathers and mothers so far apart.
Essex, Hertfordshire, Wessex, Sussex;
Hither, thither, helter-skelter.
Children perplexed as per stable site of home;
To and fro, back and forth.

## *Split Apart*

Come along, children, we must depart in hurry,
We must escape to Frances's house.
Stare not at me with doleful eyes;
It would only make me blubber and teary.

Come along, children, we must carry on regardless;
I've got you, though penniless and downtrodden.
You look so sad, I feel so crestfallen,
Life ahead so bountiful and frightless.

Come along, children, we are weary and sad.
If I could I'd turn back time.
Not your fault, do not cry in turn;
Blame the split upon your Mum and Dad.

Come along, children, we are here at last.
Split apart, we are safe at least,
In joyful tears we rejoice at least.
Pardon the split, I implore at last.

## *Siblings of Mine*

A wholesome look recently;
Revelation of amazing disparity.
Same parents, different in disposition.
These siblings of mine.

Features to fate and destiny,
Totally non-comparable.
Similarities mere gene in action.
These siblings of mine.

Scattered hither-thither, far afield;
Converged for father's burial rites.
Unfamiliar mob
These siblings of mine.

Grown with acquired temperament,
In tow with new sets of folks.
Multitude;
These siblings of mine.

Strangers each and every one;
Twenty years an awful trick.
No more brothers and sisters of yesteryears,
These siblings of mine.

## *Flock Dispersal*

Harmonious but hectic;
Family growth increasingly hectic.
Counting but one dead, all nine children,
Through tough and chaotic times,
Each other's back solidly protected.

Amiable and sturdy parents
Raised their children with care and love.
Suffered through the madness,
Adrenalin-fuelled teenage years,
Father and mother persevered.

Inevitable the dispersal of flock.
Dispersed and scattered far afield;
Only but a few remnant.
Chaotic and hectic those years gone by,
Quiet and calm the position new.

Mother Susannah affected the most,
Wondering and mulling
Positions old and new.
Either hectic or tranquil;
Her flock best protected in her coup.

## *Balderdash*

Long period gone, cue amazing transformation.
Same dialect, different manner of speech.
Kith and kin converged in ritual speech;
Ceremonial rite set in motion.

Trapped in a trance-like realm,
Afloat in a vacuous void,
Slippery slope dimension zoid.
Eerie words floating right at me:

Twaddle, twaddle, gobbledygook.
Jabber, babble, gobbledygook.
Balderdash me say gobbledygook.
Drivel, drivel, gobbledygook.

Floating back familiar voices queried,
'Are you listening gook?'
Yes, balderdash, drivel, bunkum, gobbledygook.
All eyes turned and weirdly stared.

## *Irish Sun*

Cassidy O'Caiside
Wee son of mine.
Stroke of luck,
Angelic being;
Time stood still when he arrived.
Pop! The perfect view emerged:
Pink bundle, pack of joy.
Budding star, the Irish sun;
Stroke of genius,
Wee son of mine,
Cassidy O'Caiside.

## *Noisy Sound of Silence*

Abated the discordant cacophony;
Preparation and departure of the children.
Incessant calling out of names,
Repeated impulsive name callings,
Abated the noisy din, din, din.
Our rushing up and down the stairs,
Home alone at what expense?
Over-rated companionship or what?
Grasping the blissful moment,
I drifted beyond the realm.
Mute, totally deaf and dumb;
Eerie house, noiselessly screeched
Deep in my soul as I wandered through and through,
Meddling, the telephone shrilled out in anger,
Exploding the noisy sound of silence.
Drifting back from beyond the realm,
Two ears popped and were assaulted
By the natter natter from the other side.

## *Dire Strait*

Horror!
Death so gloomy;
Overcast the grey slate of heaven.
Hollow!
Death so roomy;
Creation of death the empty space.
Sorrow!
Death so sullen;
The stricken heart of mine.

Dismay!
Death so dire;
Dreadful the dreadfulness of death.
Distraught!
Death so disastrous;
Marshy quagmire the quandary of death.
Good grief!
Death so grievous;
The grieving heart of mine.

Dire strait!
The marshy quagmire;
Perched on the balancing scale.
Our faith in hereafter the anchor,
We mourn the passing equally.
We equally celebrate the led fruitful life,
Grief-stricken mourners.
In solemn mood shall we proclaim
Adieu until we meet again.

*Requiem for Sir Nicholas.*

## *My Family of Choice*

In your giant embrace,
As my steps retrace,
Marching in trident pace,
Onward, forward, toward purity.
Entwining our spiritual disparity,
Clinging to new-found sorority,
We did partake in grace.
In your warmth embrace
My family of choice!

Death may thrust its jagged dagger
Dust may entomb the empty armour,
Deep within this black bird's core,
Your essence lives on unharmed.
Epitome of purity saintly hemmed.
Chance 'n' mischance, perchance more hugs still,
As we abide in disparate sleep.
In God's own embrace,
My family of choice!

*Dedicated to Peggy Porter who died recently*

# Part Four

# The Reluctant Mistress

*Contents*

## *The Reluctant Mistress*

Do not French kiss me;
A peck on the cheek is enough.

Do not French kiss me;
Can I have a hug instead?

What's the point of cooking if the restaurants are serving?
What's the point of cooking if your wife and kids are serving?

Do not touch me;
My bed is meant for sleeping.

Do not touch me;
My house is not an inn.

## *Desperate Miss Basset*

No dinners and trappings;
The pounds will only pile on.
No late night pub-crawling;
Our livers deserve better than that.
No incessant shopping for clothes and shoes;
They wear off with age.
A house next to a lake is all one expects.
Situated in Scotland, Loch Lomond the favourite choice of place.
If one cannot afford Loch Lomond and a house,
One needs to rethink his priority in life.
One has not enough money to maintain his concubines.
How on earth is one able to keep and maintain
Desperate Miss Basset?

## *Tally-Ho*

Respect begets respect;
Go home, I bid you adieu.
Disrespect begets disrespect;
Tally-ho.
You are such an idiot.

## *Flip Around – Get a Grip*

He loves her; she loves him not.
She loathes him; he loathes her not.
Flip around, get a grip.
Get a grip, show some respect.
Appraise her not with dozy eyes;
Appraise her not with mouth agape.
Cast your eyes on her ugly face;
Cast your eyes on her saggy boobs.
Get a grip.
Respect yourself.

## *Who's Fooling Whom?*

Erica must have a clue, she is not dumb.
Time and time again you disappear.
You seldom appear with woeful tales,
Hoping to confuse and convince her that you are still together.

Erica must have a hint, she is not blind.
Ever so often you take a trip abroad,
Dragging your dutiful but beautiful secretary along with you,
Bearing expensive gifts on your return.

Erica is neither blind nor dumb,
She is all clued up and a smart alec.
She detests you so much and lives with hope.
She wills you on to take even more trips abroad.

Do you really know your wife?
She is always miserable about your seldom stint at home,
Always casts the gifts straight into the trash can.
Your presence messes up her new-found life.

Your purported brother is the incumbent Mr Diouf.
Now who's fooling whom, Mr Diouf?

## *Soliloquy*

I'm not sleeping with her but will let people
Believe otherwise.

Do not intend to sleep with him.
Bizarrely I like the attention.

What can I to do to change the situation, though?
Gifts I have given. Gifts I intend to give.

Do not intend to sleep with him.
Bizarrely I like the attention.

Loving, caring and attentive I will be.
Perseverance is my motto.

## *Quid Pro Quo*

The empty seats speak loud and clear enough:
You do not have friends to call your own.
With all your wealth and prosperity in life,
You lay in death all but a lonely corpse.
Your embittered wife is present here in mourning;
Your resentful children are all present in grief.
Where are all your hangers-on and sycophants?
Where is your golden mistress?
T'is with all pleasure that we inform you, sir,
She resolved that whilst you lay in state
T'is a joyful day for a
Golden spa.
Quid pro quo,
You reap what you sow.

## *Back in Time*

We heard you've made the leap back in time.
You've gone eventually far away.
Hooray to that and you we say.
We encourage that you stay away.
No more groping when she says otherwise;
No more hands and legs all over the place.
You mope and grope about in vain;
You whimper and simper like a sick dog in heat,
Demanding to be loved but to no avail.
You finally saw the inequality of the whole affair;
The unrequited sickening fabled affair,
The artful manipulator by your side,
We are proud of ourselves, so you must be too.
We finally got rid of the grope and sycophant;
We made a leap jointly back in time.

# Part Five
# Fabled Affairs

*Contents*

## *Straight from the Heart*

Beloved Ollie Jones,
Rejoice, you are much loved indeed.
An adorable and gentle knob head,
Never love someone dearly like so.
Intoxicating, your sweet love;
Abounds on and on.
Heart and soul to Ollie Jones.

The soul suggests that I let it be.
Must endeavour to ignore the soul.
Body aches in vain for warmth;
The warmth of thy lovely arms.
Never there to fulfil the need;
Heart aches and jolts in pain.
The mere thought of Ollie Jones.

Forever the wait at a distance,
Continually inducing your spirit.
Ollie Jones, Ollie Jones;
Until you come crawling
Hither back to me,
Straight from my heart
To one, adorable, Mr Ollie Jones.

## *Father Drew*

Hear my secret lament,
My mantras and chants.
We are worthy a wife to be.
Do not dilly dally,
Wait no longer than necessary.
The heart recites in prayer
The incessant mantras and chants.

Married to your course;
Difficult to fight one's rival,
The sovereign ruler of the universe;
Quick divorce from God.
Man of the cloth,
Say a little mass for me,
Whilst I recite my mantras and chants.

## *Wild Goose Chase*

She searched to no avail,
Love and affection alluring;
She found two geese in the end,
Geese already been taken.

One ardently devoted;
By his side a gander.
Other ardently devoted;
The Lord most-high betrothed.

Wild goose chase with perseverance;
Passionately she persists,
Hoping that one may backslide.
Nigh on.

## *Harlem Paradigm*

Consider this hypothesis:
One asks of you, dear Ollie,
Leave Jo Beth as you promised,
Come live with me in Harlem.

Jo Beth wants you not
For lack of love on your own part,
You continually say.
You both deserve a break in galaxies far apart.

Come to my galaxy;
Harlem is pleasant,
Harlem is fun,
Harlem is perpetually endearing.

Survey this premise
We shall together indeed.
Whilst the cat is out of the bag,
Come stay a while in Harlem.

We've been together for eternity;
Eternal choice selection time.
Jo Beth goes back to whence she came,
Whilst you stay with me in Harlem.

## *Fool in Love*

Such a fool in love.
Blind to the fact
He loves her not.
A friend he is but not a game.

Go back from whence you came;
Retract,
Retreat,
Forever keep your distance.

Be courageous, chérie,
Be assertive, chérie,
He may grow to love you one day
If you love him less today.

## *Unrequited Love*

She loves him like no other.
Unrequited love, like most other,
He whispers lascivious obscenities like no other.
Moments she embellishes like most other.
He sends mixed signals like no other.
He promises to hold her once more tomorrow;
But tomorrow never comes.

# Part Six

## Some Friends Indeed

*Contents*

## *Foe*

Who needs enemies
When they have a friend like you?
She was so sensitive and fragile
When she cried to you for help.
When you offered your hand in friendship
She grabbed with all her might.
She felt as happy as one can be.

Her spirit lifted,
Some colour appeared on her faded cheeks.
Dark shadow around her eyes
Began to fade away.
She became more determined.
She reciprocated the friendship.
You were entrusted with all her affairs.

Like adversary the devil you are,
You took away your friendship.
She cries herself to sleep most nights.
Dark shadow around her eyes
Appears darker than ever.
It hurts so much coming from you;
She trusted you the most.

## *A Friend Indeed*

It is too wonderful to know
You are in my life today.
Standing with you, I regain my confidence.
Standing with you, I regain my poise.
Therefore to thee I strive to embrace
My very good friend indeed.
It is too wonderful to know that;
I am not alone today.

*Dear Janet.*

## *Eyes Wide Open*

Forsaken by my bosom pal;
Abandoned in an empty ditch.
Stumbling alone in darkness;
Floundering for the glorious exit
With my eyes shut in pain.
Seeking the way out of this dungeon,
My brain foggy and mushy.

Abandoned in an abyss;
Who's here to set me free?
All alone but the clinging shadow.
Floundering for the glorious exit
With my head pulsating in pain.
Seeking the elusive Northern light,
Come on, foggy and mushy brain.

Do concentrate, O mushy brain;
The only tool this point in time.
The guiding light, the Northern light;
Need to locate and work the switch.
We must focus the tool, and I
Need to crawl out of this ditch
With my eyes wide open.

## *The Silent Caller*

Who's that on the phone for the umpteenth time?
The silent and menacing calls again.
Chums for as far back as I can remember;
Did every little thing together.
Shared and shared alike;
Bathing to eating to sleeping together,
Completed each other's sentences at times.
A flair people thought was spooky.

Then she met and fell for Danny;
She sternly refused to share their bed.
*What happens to me now?* I thought.
Left on the shelf to rot and be cast aside.
Got myself in their bed somehow.
He extended his love to me, of course.
When she answered the phone once more,
I hung up the receiver in disdain.

Mine at last to keep;
Vehemently I refused to share our bed.
Left on the shelf to rot and be cast aside,
Now who's there on the phone for the umpteenth time?
The silent and menacing calls again.
'Hello? Hello?
Veronica? Is that you?
I guess you want your husband back.'

## *Non Raison d'Être*

Friends are there without a cause;
Without a cause or beneficial intent;
Friends are there when we need them most;
Friends exist and are here at ease.

Angels exist and are here to impress
Our earthly life-form; friendly beings,
They come to us without a cause,
Sent to us in times of wretchedness.

When we receive angelic friends
Life becomes bearable in full.
Bearable life worth living in full.
Non raison d'être my friend Vicks.

*To Vicky Robertson – an angelic friend.*

## *Needless Flight*

Flight to thee;
No respite.
Submerged in turbulence;
No respite.
Useless the needless flight.
Needless the useless friendship.

Thy help in desperation;
Not forthcoming.
Rally round I pray;
To no avail.
Useless the needless lament.
Needless the useless friendship.

## *Tulip*

Emblem of Holland, tulip.
Not a second thought.
Never stopped to smell the tulip
In the wild.
What's the point?
Behold the prominent garden lot:
Roses, carnations, daffodils, Daphne Wakeling.

Gifted with a bunch.
On second thought
Did stop and smelt the tulip.
Long green petals, pink, yellow, bulbous buds asleep.
Awakened to most beautiful blossom.
Quintessential tulip amongst the prominent garden lot;
Roses, carnations, daffodils, Daphne Wakeling.

*A single bloom from the whole bunch. Dear Daphne.*

## *Potted Geranium*

Kathy Eaton delivered a potted geranium,
Erupting from the seeds of her lovely heart.
Commiserations read each petal.
Town councillor in making;
Legal eagle in mid-flight.
Convoluted with emotion my heart erupted,
Blissful pieces quavered in acknowledging pendulum.

Bless her lovely heart and geranium;
At last, confirmation!
Our concave hill has eyes.
Balling at us always;
Confirmation at last!
In figurative shape of this lovely sweetheart,
Kathy Eaton delivered a potted geranium.

## *Too Little Too Early*

My shortcomings;
The shameful side of me.
Only but a friend dares
To let me into the white lies.
If there is a friend in you,
It is too little too early to tell.
Tell me all, I dare you.
A little while longer;
A friend or foe,
The truth lies within.
Too little too early to tell either way.

## *Neighbourly Deeds*

Earthly rich not me per se;
Spiritually rich, adorned in gold.
Neighbourly folks to the rescue in queue,
Fair trio ladies; fair indeed.
Manifesting kindness all in fold,
Pining pounding heart at ease,
Pruning shrubbery all at ease,
Harvested veggies token in fold,
Resounding neighbourly deeds indeed.
Family Wells the first in queue,
All spiritually rich, adorned in gold;
Manifesting kindness clear to see.

*With all my heart to the next-door Wells:*
*Ann, Pauline and Eileen.*

# *Part Seven*

# *Flora and Fauna*

*Contents*

## *Epping*

Epping. My beautiful Epping.
Set in the middle of immeasurable forest,
Miles and miles of greens and trees;
Picturesque acres of the forest
Is such a lovely sight to see.
Ghostly white and serene in winter snow;
All shades of the rainbow the autumn leaves;
Walk for miles in summer months;
Spring is the best season of them all.
Soon as we arrived I knew for sure
One is home at last.

## *Wither Thou Africa*

Wither thou Africa;
The land of diamond and oil
Had the best of everything;
Could not survive for fraud and scam.

Fabled land of the rising sun,
What have they done to you?
Unrecognisable land of honey and gold,
Poverty stricken land of disease.

Ravaged by its unscrupulous leaders and the led;
No more the source of nectar,
No more the source of gold and oil,
No more the land I knew and loved.

Wither thou Africa;
Cradle of civilization.
The universe watches in amazement
As you wither and perish.

## *Through My Gaping Windows*

How magnificent a sight to behold
Each waking morning;
Vast open miles of green field to the front,
Thriving yonder to eternity.

Quaint modest garden to the rear,
Full of chirping birds dancing to nature's acoustic tune.
Not a hint of noise at bay,
Not a trace of crowd in sight.

What a wonderful sight to behold
Each waking morning.
Through the gaping windows of
My little Epping house.

## *Violet Afrique*

Intoxicatingly beautiful at dawn and dusk,
How beautiful a place to be, Africa.
Surveying the horizon as the sun goes down;
How very beautiful the sun rays and hope.
Surveying the horizon as the sun emerges;
How menacingly beautiful,
Intoxicatingly beautiful as the gods expect.
Sunrise, sunset, dawn, or dusk;
So rich in powerful colours the sun rays.
How mesmerising the colourful sight;
Palm fronds scatter the colourful sunrays and hope.
Violet, indigo, cerulean, violet;
What mesmerising sight indeed.

In between dawn and dust, bedlam,
The earth opens and spurts out the maddening crowd.
Every nook and cranny crammed and swamped,
Noise, noise, abuse my ears.
Stifling heat is the worst to bear;
Hunger pangs, hunger pangs.
Stomach lining eating itself
All day long, for what seems long.
I must escape, I must escape.
Lo and behold it is the handsome dusk
Hankering for the beautiful dawn.
Violet, indigo, cerulean, violet;
What mesmerising rays of vision and hope indeed.

*To Rosalind, with all my love.*

## *Nature's Own Lullaby in African Hinterland*

As darkness swiftly crawls and envelopes the sky lark,
Soon after the sky becomes pitch dark,
Surrounding bushes come alive with discordant cacophony
Creepy crawlies, frogs 'n' toads in ill-orchestrated symphony.
Chirping crickets in direct competition with croaky frogs 'n' toads
In dug-out swampy lay-bys.
Rest assured nature's own lullaby
Slumber time deep in African hinterland.

Do not count sheep for forty winks
Pay no heed to stinging mosquito bites 'n' nicks
Tune in to discordant critters as each shrilly shrieks.
Pay attention to the croaky calls of frogs 'n' toads in heat,
Accept the weird composition of this nightly unmusical treat,
Immerse yourself deep in it as you drift
As you catch forty winks, nod off to
Nature's own lullaby deep in African hinterland.

# Part Eight
# Playground Jingles

*Contents*

## *Beyond the Pale*

Insufferable woman. Oh yes you are.

T is nag nag nag.
T is tut tut tut.
T is din din din.

Argument and kerfuffle all the time,
Can't stand the hustle and bustle, not one more time.
Hubbub! Hullabaloo! Baa humbug!

T is din din din.
T is tut tut tut.
T is nag nag nag.

Insufferable woman. Oh yes you are.

Beyond the pale!

## *Hoi Polloi*

Hoi polloi are marching en masse,
Marching en route towards your end.
Take the child and run to the hills;
Hoi polloi are marching en masse.
Take the child and make it quick,
Make it quick to save your lives,
Make it quick to change the world.
Hoi polloi are coming en route,
You must escape. You must escape.
You must escape to save the child,
You must escape to save the world.
Save the child. You save the world.
Hoi polloi are here en masse.

## *Silly Sally*

Habba Silly Sally;
What a funny story.
Sister Millie Silly?
Silly Millie 'n' Sally.
Mammie 'n' Pappie must be gutted.
Habba Silly Sally.

## *Doppelgänger*

Mirror me: mirror you
Mirror image spit at us.
Spit at us: spit at us
Spitting image you and I.
Doppel doppel, we are alike.
Gänger gänger, we are alike.
Doppelgänger you and I.

# Part Nine

# Fantasy World

*Contents*

## *The Bell Tolled*

When the nuns opened the gate, we rushed down to the brook.
Discarding our clothes, we dove into the glistening water.
Heaven on earth, it was so right and soothing;
We dove and swam and dove some more.
The gods called and I answered.

When I dove the last time, I went through a cavity;
The legendary underwater gate to heaven or hell.
Trapped and gasping for air,
Totally blind, I could not see through the muddy water in the chasm,
In a foetal position I crawled around in confusion.

Could not find my bearing or the exit;
I started gulping water and knew I was drowning.
I heard a bell tolling in the distance.
Then I started to recite our lady's prayer:
'Hail Mary, full of grace, the lord is with thee. Blessed—'

Heavenly calm and beautiful; I could feel a presence.
A hand grabbed and shoved me up through the orifice of the abyss;
Standing at the brook bank were my friends and the nuns.
Aghast and horror-struck, they gawked as my body reappeared and floated.
When the referee blew his whistle, they let out a cry of relief.

A hand scooped me out of the water,
Proceeded to pump the trapped water out of my system.
The bell stopped tolling when I opened my eyes.
'Why was the bell tolling, am I dead?'
'What bell?' Sister Maria Gorathie enquired.

'You have been gone for two hours!' they all cried in unison.

## *The Fairy*

Occupying a sixth floor apartment.
Awakened one fateful morning by a soft nudge,
Overwhelmed by the most beautiful light,
I watched in awe as the walls glow with the rainbow light.
How enthralling and fascinating.

I followed willingly without a second thought.
When it entered the kitchen, I followed at a pace.
The message was loud and clear:
Perched on the kitchen window,
Charlene, nearly two years old, about to fall off the ledge.

I reached to snatch but tripped and fell instead,
I cried out for help as I fell.
Heard the most peculiar sound:
*Fphleep!* Then she was in my arms.
Cradling her in disbelief, I thanked the invincible force.

Pointing towards the kitchen door, she said,
'Mummy, look, a fairy, a big fairy!'
'There is nothing there,' I corrected.
She turned and said almost to herself:
*'She has gone now, put me down Mummy.'*

Just then, the song 'I Believe in Angels' came on the radio.
What a coincidence.

## *Enigma*

Whilst recuperating in Withington hospital,
I received daily visits from a strange young lady.
She sat on a chair next to my bed and sang me the same odd song.
She never changed the tune or the song's content.
I looked forward to her visit in the early hours of each morning.
In her soft doleful voice, she sang each time:

*It is totally an enigma,*
*The riddle of the trapped damsel.*
*Her foolish father sold her to the greedy husband,*
*Who in turn sacrificed her for the money's worth.*
*When they ask, tell them that Angelina is dead but trapped,*
*Planted in a big pot in the room with padlock and key.*
*Open the door, Angelina wants to go home.*
*Angelina Alfalfa wants to go home.*

She failed to turn up the last morning;
No one remembered her when I enquired.
I was overcome with sadness as I sat in the wheelchair ready to go.
I didn't even say thanks for her hospitality. *Goodbye*, I thought.
Just then, a gush of wind blew a window open,
An old newspaper page landed on my lap.
The caption read, 'Angelina Alfalfa still missing two years on.
Contact the central police station if you have any information.'

## *Dreamy State*

Major operation booked for gastric and peptic ulcer.
A lengthy slash from upper thorax through to the abdomen.
She went into the hospital without my knowledge;
That night I tossed and turned, waiting for her return.

I must have drifted off somewhat;
Then she appeared, looking deathly ashen and doubled over.
She beckoned with both hands without uttering a word,
With her mouth still shut, she asked if I was ready.

'Ready for what?' I asked in absolute confusion.
'You must come with me at once; the lift is ready and waiting.'
'No, mother, we are not ready yet,' I screamed.
Just then, the light came on and my father appeared.

My mother had been here a moment ago, I cried to him.
'She could not have been here and in the operating theatre.'
He reassured me it was just a dream.
I mulled over the strangeness of it all for the rest of the night.

When we arrived at the hospital the next morning,
Mother was still in and out of consciousness.
She opened her eyes at one stage; clutching my hand, she whispered,
'No, we are not ready at all. The lift can depart without us.'

## *The Vanishing Mist*

An apparition or figment of my imagination?
About to nod off when the nudging and pulling began.
I sat up in utter dismay and looked around, bewildered.
Only but a mist hovered at the bottom of the bed;
A mist hovering inside a heated room, unbelievable.
It hovered, jived and undulated wildly.
Intensely I watched, captivated but spooked.
Pulled myself together after a while and turned on the bedside light.
In a flash, the mist vanished – *poof!* The snuffling noise was clear.
About to nod off again, I turned off the bedside light.
Almost immediately my legs were pulled and nudged,
The mist jived and undulated more wildly than before;
Was that you, father, what message do you bear?
If only I could decipher the lingo of the jiving mist.
Do come again, father, I am willing to learn
The lingua franca of the jiving vanishing mist.

## *The Final Rococo Party*

We threw the rococo party again last night, the king and I.
Quite extravagantly and ornately attired,
I sat in full regalia on my throne next to the king.
Bowing and unassuming, the citizens approached and paid homage.
With a flick of hand I ordered them away.
They seemed not to pay much attention
To my disdain; the procession carried on regardless.
The prince approached and sat on me despite my disapproval.
The children wailed for no apparent reason;
I signalled in vain to make them stop.
Then I noticed the open casket. I turned to the king and smiled nicely.
'Darling, instruct the guards to remove the dreadful ornate casket.
How inappropriate and sacrilegious,
A casket in our baroque party.'
His eyes were oddly moist with dewdrops, perchance.
I stood up in my finery and approached the casket.
A quick glimpse inside revealed a blasphemous misdeed;
Mummified and dolled up to the nines, I lay in eternal slumber.

## *Knock Knock*

Two sharp knocks each time.
Acquainted and used to the mysterious knocks,
I perceived them as the completion of each successful day.
Tried in the past to locate the source without success.
Today was no exception; the knocks came at twelve midnight prompt.
It was a dark moonless night and the wind was fiercely blowing.
I shut some shutters to moderate the temperature of the room.
Bang bang, the remaining shutters danced about in the wind.
*Might as well close them all*, I said to myself.
Leant over the bed to reach the remaining window.
A clap of thunder and extended flash of lightning;
He was standing there in white flowing apparel.
Window with no ledge, how could anyone project so high up?
On close inspection, it became apparent;
Dumbstruck, I suppressed a scream.
'Let me in, I am cold.' he cajoled and begged.
'I have been knocking for months on end.'
'You are dead, Mr Simms, you can't come in,' I heard myself repeating.
Knock knock, bang bang; it went on till I heard the cocks crowing at dawn.

## *The Golden Ball*

We entered the gully at last after trekking for what
seemed ages.
We marvelled at the vastness of it and cowered in the
darkness.
Then the golden ball appeared as they assured us,
Sitting there on the horizon, daring us to move.
We stopped and stared in amazement for what
seemed ages.
When the church bell struck twelve o'clock midnight,
We panicked and started to disperse.
The golden ball hovering above us followed at the
same pace.
We were amazed and burst into trot and ran;
When we reached the first row of houses,
We screamed with all our strength for help.
The elders came running with their lit 'clair-de-lune'.
'You have been to the gully seeking out the golden
ball,' they admonished.
'Regardez!' they laughed.
'It is only the moon.'

## *Regression*

Prince Imagie was on board the chariot as it thundered past.
The raggedy and tattered man stumbled and nearly fell.
When the chariot paused at the exit, the scruffy man approached,
Stretched his hand and beseeched the prince,
'Pray thee, sir, give us some crumbs.'

'Why, pray tell, should one give thee crumbs?
Vanish to the fields and carry on with thy assigned task.'
The shabby man stood his ground and stared directly at the prince;
Like a fiery dagger, the words came out of the bushy mouth,
Stabbed and twisted jaggedly at Prince Imagie's heart:

'Thou art so pompous and frivolous, sir.
Let the truth be known today and always;
Hither stands thy real father.
When the king failed in his duty, one was there to do the honours,
Sired thy mother who begot thee.'

Prince Imagie took his sword and sliced off his father's unkempt head;
Ran till the palace gate, thumped and banged till the king appeared.
'Pray thee, tell who are you?' the king bellowed.
She woke up in perspiration and sighed;
The recurring dream yet again.

# Part Ten
# Mixed Bag of Thoughts

*Contents*

## *Purgatory*

Halfway motel to heaven or hell,
Only but an illusion.
Illusion totally shattered.
Already in purgatory here on earth;
The truth be known and told to all.
No hereafter halfway motel to heaven or hell;
We must atone and change our ways,
We must converge and amend our ways;
We are in purgatory here and now.
Straight to heaven or hell when we depart;
The last call for atonement, here and now.
All on board. All on board.
Get on board the train to heaven or hell.

## *Snide Comment*

Tongue-in-cheek, that snide comment.
Jagged edges; the dagger
Destroys the essence of me,
Does nothing to change your image.
A colossal ogre,
A dreadful bully,
Readily eager to destroy another.

Never sure what you are implying;
Not really bothered,
Several ogres to deal with.
Insinuations to decipher;
Bite your tongue and swallow the bile.
Better still, be clever,
Produce a productive advice.

## *Miss Givens*

One does not have a choice, she has reservations.
She is suspicious of any act of kindness.
After years of ill treatment and cruelty,
She crawled out of her cocoon;
Matured Miss Qualms.

Do not blame her for having reservations.
Consumed with doubt, she is suspicious of your intention.
After years of disrespect and neglect,
She crawled out of her carapace;
Matured Miss Givens.

## *Hang About*

Amble and dawdle, no need to hurry.
Drag your feet to your heart's content.
Dilly dally for England for all I care;
Shilly shally with no hope in sight.
Ready or not, I'll be gone
In a jiffy.

## *Why Oh Why*

Were you there when the incidents occurred?
Why oh why
Do you swallow all hook, line and sinker?
To each incident different factions;
A lot depends on the interpreter,
Right thinking member of the society.

Were you there when the alleged sins were committed?
Why oh why
Do you bear false witness?
To each occurrence different factions;
A lot depends on the perception of the
Right thinking member of the society.

Were you there when the alleged offences were committed?
Why oh why
Do you hunt and persecute?
Judge not expeditiously;
The best judgement is done judiciously by the
Right thinking members of the society.

## *Pipe Dream*

Psychosis habitually in parity with fantasy,
Sheer wishful thinking
Compared to reality.
You are, at most, insane.
One more castle in Spain last night.
Quirky little castles in the air,
Inhabited by the pixies.
A bunch gathered around
Whilst visiting Elvis.
Whilst in conversation with God,
St Peter emerged,
Announced that the roof
Above the East Wing is leaking.
Chuckling to myself, I thought,
'The roof is not the only thing leaking,
Your brain has been leaking for a while,
It may be empty as we speak.
Hurry up with the next castle;
You ought to finish before dusk.'

## *Keep Silent*

Silence is the best answer in conflict.
Silence is golden at loggerheads.
Silence is an admission of guilt at variance.
It costs dearly to keep silence at odds.

Steadfastly she keeps shtum.

Probabilities abound.
No response, she is innocent.
No response, she is oblivious.
Oblivious of the alleged hurtful deeds.

Repositions abound.
Bring to her attention the hurtful deeds,
The inappropriate conduct that annoys you most.
Air your views directly or for ever keep your peace.

## *Evelyn*

Mysterious and elusive; the world hunts Evelyn.
With impudence and effrontery she lives her life,
Amazed and perplexed about her popularity.
Heads constantly scratched in awe;
Such audacity, such bravery.

She converses in the privacy of her home,
The world reacts and answers back.
How peculiar the dramatic and spectacular life.
She makes a move, the world jumps to attention.
Watching her every step and action.

Fuelling the need for private eyes,
Wrong interpretations of her every act.
Billboards posted for her consumption,
Telephone bugged and hidden cameras in place.
Unflinching and unperturbed she presses on.

With all due respect, I bow to Evelyn.
My hat is unendingly doffed to Evelyn.
She may have cried hopelessly for truce,
She may have bemoaned her past misfortune;
The newfound bravado is worthy of emulation.

## *Chutzpah*

The ghastly lady in attendance,
Apprehensive and full of trepidation.
Forlornly I looked on,
Ill-mannered anecdotes sprayed at me.

The audience she sought was forced at me;
In desperate attempt, she bared her ill-shaped gnashers.
Trapped, unable to leave the room *tout de suite*
Ill-mannered, uncouth clichés came tumbling at me.

Endlessly she droned on and on,
Mocked and teased the way I speak.
Woefully failed to master the exotic accent;
Plucked up courage in the end, I let it be known:

Ignorant, unintelligent, O ghastly lady,
Celebrate not thy stupidity;
An alien from another galaxy.
English is my third language at heart.

## *Retribution Day*

I hope for the glorious day,
The day of retribution and justice.
Heart filled with grief today
Will overflow with joy.
The day of reckoning.

I pine for the glorious day,
The day of reprisal and vengeance.
Calamitous life of yesterday
Replaced with radiant *joie de vivre.*
The vengeful day.

I wait for the glorious day,
The day that the gods have specially chosen.
Sad and lonely with no succour in sight;
Joyfully wed to an Irish god.
The retribution day.

## *Bon Voyage*

In state you lay
Whilst we sip and gulp your chosen treacle.
Were you here, merrily you would imbibe,
Sip and gulp your chosen treacle,
Smiling peacefully in stupor state,
Secrets best known to you.

In death you lay
Akin to the pose in stupor state.
Smiling to more secrets than ever.
Formaldehyde the embalming fluid, or sherry?
Same difference.
Ever so tranquil and calm the eternal rest.

## *Battle of Might and Will*

Where can we stand for this raging battle?
A neutral and common podium
Where all and sundry can bear witness.
Ambushed position not fair as it stands.
Hidden behind the shadow, you strike at will
With perfect vision of my every move.
My weakness to nakedness,
My heart in full display,
You poke away mercilessly.

Courageous and eager to retaliate but
You are invisible.
Cowards, lily-livered and gutless.
Behind each other you are invincible.
All alone but ready to battle if the setting is fair.
Take a pose at the visible podium
Where all and sundry can judge the fight.
You have the might.
I have the will.

## *Flip-Sided Love*

Inexplicable sweet love;
The scale,
The complexity,
The evergreen greenery and trees.
Ever-flowing field of peace,
Babbling brook,
Cascading water,
Peaceful sighs,
Clear blue sparkling sky,
Sprinkles of freshly sewn clouds,
Syrupy juicy love.

Inexplicable bitter love;
The enormity,
The strain,
Gangrenous lifeless trees.
Dead leaves litter strewn,
Percolating brook,
Recycled,
Putrid water lake,
Treacherous sky,
Cyclonic desert storm,
Soured acidic love.

## *Single Stem*

Aver not vacuous promises,
Avow not the globe.
The earth too wide to encapsulate
Single stem of rose so red.
Redeemable, the pink glowing cheek.

Promise not your soul,
Swear not your life away,
An oath too vague to encapsulate
Single stem of lily so white.
Redeemable, love so pure.

## *Frabian War*

Acclaimed citizens of Frabia;
Kudos each and every one.
Keep the evil sprite alive,
The misery of the Frabian war.
Fresh and septic scabs unhealed,
Dead heroes, living dead heroes
Living in new recruits at most.
At variance with the world at large.

Multicultural children of the civil war;
Kwashiorkor ridden bags of bones.
Sparsely clad in raggedy clothes,
Recall the nefarious property seizures.
Miserly twenty, miserly pound,
All present had to start afresh.
Kudos each and every one;
Acclaimed citizens of Frabia.

## *Unfair World*

Weld together in a composite whole,
The melting pot, the earth.
Amalgamation of everything equal;
Some more equal than others.
All different forces that differentiate all.

Chance or destiny,
Everything so relative.
Some more relative than others;
The ignominy, the humiliation of it all.
Sparrows soar over the eagles.

## *Paranoia*

A cankerworm
Gnaws through the entire being,
Befuddles the sensory organisms,
The mind, the thinking faculty.
Paranoia, parasitic leech,
Reinforces befuddlement.
The protagonist ever so apprehensive.

Succinct observation, if I may:
Paranoia, a vital key,
Opens gate to wild debate,
Heightens awareness,
Wariness, self-mistrust and doubt.
Paranoid protagonist
In her own fantastic world.

## *Goldfish*

In an aquarium floats thou,
A goldfish.
Not so golden,
Nude, without scaly flesh.
Twirling around claustrophobic pool,
Nowhere to hide.

In an aquarium floats thou,
A mermaid.
Without the beauty or
Graceful flairs.
Not a pretty sight,
Not a hiding place.

In an aquarium floats thou;
Live on stage,
The watchful world.
Such intrusion,
Total invasion,
Ill at ease as you squirm.

## *A Penny, a Piece*

A million fold plus
A penny, a piece,
Makes one a millionaire.
Counting periodically the times.
One has been fed the evil line,
A single sentence says it all,
'Where are you from?'

The inquiring minds
Declaring the difference in us.
Tactfully or tactlessly,
The queries, however fashioned,
Inflict separatist idealism;
Disintegration of the society,
From the aliens amongst us.

## *Eerie Rendezvous*

Lost in the booming eerie sound,
Floating in the tuneful flowing wind,
Gyrating and floating away our innocence.
Akin to the lilies of the valley's essence;
We coupled and gyrated with reckless abandon,
Frenzied gyration till early dawn.

Virgin babes 'n' gods
The treaty dance,
Engulfed by rays of the silvery moon.
We surrendered in blissful ecstatic moan;
The eerie dance so exhilarating,
The frenzied moves so exhausting.

Spent heap spread out in the coven,
Entwined and artistically woven.
Babes 'n' gods famished in file homeward,
Gyrating to the tuneful whirlwind.
The early frost bites back to senses,
In anticipation for the next rendezvous.

*Eerie Rendezvous (sketch by Stephen Parkinson)*

## *Sign Readers*

Emblazoned invisibly,
Thick on my forehead,
The mysterious inscription:
Kick me further,
Already in the dumps.

The clandestine treaty
Converged the entities and I.
Faces known and unknown,
The forces that be;
Invisible sign readers.

Undetectable to me,
The sign to them radiates.
Incessant bid to erase
Wrinkles the natural ridges further,
Whilst the etch remains.

## *Curse Be*

A spell from one to all,
Curse be.
The tongue, the mouth, the whole being.
Devil-possessed minions
That spread false allegations.
Until you retract your falsities,
Curse be.

A spell from one to all,
Curse be.
The tongue, the mouth, the whole being.
Devil's advocates
Who dwell on trumped up allegations.
Until you undo the hurt,
Curse be.

Dismiss this not as an empty spell,
For God is my witness.
The divine interventionist
Curses the flippant hurtful tongue.
Until the hurt's undone,
Until you unchain my heart,
Curse be unto you.

## *The Magic Wand*

Wave the magic wand
Whilst there's still life in us.
In time to live and laugh in time,
Spare not the magic wand,
Lest we crumble to rise no more.

Wave the magic wand
Whilst the night is young at heart.
In time to walk and run in time,
Spare not the magic wand,
Lest we sleep to wake no more.

## *One Heartbeat*

Through the thin muslin cloth
Clinging flimsily over one's chest,
Clearly demarcated the two shapely mounds,
Delicately heaving at each heartbeat.
Aorta, the veins, the blood-pumping capillaries,
Seriously at work the nature's assigned role.
Thumping, never ceasing, the nature's way of life.

Caprice the seizure of one's beating heart.
The nature's other intent and plan,
The stillness of time at death,
Whilst riding the stormy life.
Died to rejuvenate the fleeting world,
One heartbeat ceases hither,
One heart begins to beat thither.

## *Easy Tiger*

The tiger charged towards us;
Stopped a nano-centimetre away.
Momentarily, we died of absolute fear;
Right in front of our very eyes,
Dissipated into tiny fragments, the tiger,
Each piece roared and mingled with the others,
Wildly pulsating, illusion-like,
Atomically charged, the pieces soldered, forming a sphinx.

The sphinx charged towards us,
Dropped a nano-centimetre away.
Roared loudly as we shook,
Right in front of our very eyes;
Easy tiger, you got me,
Mugs of cappuccino at work undoubtedly;
Way too many to count.
Move aside though, tiger-headed performing sphinx.

## *Alas! O Rotund Priest*

Rotund the she-priest;
Dog collar, habit, alb and all.
Demanded and got divided attention
In parlance – with the others she stood.
Mostly for my ears and benefit she spoke;
Made no particular sense to those that gathered.
To her other audience, she waffled aimlessly,
To my amazement she hits the target effortlessly.
Badly festered words so unpriestly.
Alas! O rotund priest;
Mind boggles,
What if thou hath no dog collar?

Not today, never again,
The badly festered chalice to thy self.
Stations of the Cross for Jesus H Christ;
If the walk be for thy sake,
I'll walk five miles the other way.
Thy ungodly mutterings so vile,
Sheer disturbance to the holy stations;
Thou might be dragged to hell muttering,
Dog collar, habit, alb and all.
Alas! O rotund priest;
Mind boggles,
What if thou hath no dog collar?

## *Silo Effect*

Not purist,
Not even the least.
Sardonic and scornful, she mounted the pulpit,
Tumbling down purulent words resounding,
Hurtful clangers accusing worshippers of social ladder climbing;
Illogical words of an impious atheist,
Penchant not befitting an ordained clergy head.

Retract thy wobbly ladder, tiny one,
Impious priest of tiny faith.
Focus not above the silo atheist view;
Theist lateral thinking more like.
Clear view from an aesthetic dimension,
Aisle one, pew three and chanting,
When has the pulpit become thy personal podium?

## *Leave Off*

It does not always follow;
What you see not always what it seems.
To you twas pink pina colada,
Twas pineapple juice in vial-like glass.

It does not always follow;
What you see not always what it seems.
To you twas black onyx gem aglow,
Twas jaded amber ashen soot.

It makes no difference what you see;
Clinically challenged your mind set.
Nearly blind you can vaguely see,
Leave off, the world can do without your sight.

## *Goodwill Tidings*

Down by the seaside,
We await the eventide
That brings the goodwill tidings,
Always from your sidings.

As the tide subsides,
We collect the cockles left aside.
Extracting the goodwill tidings,
Discarding the crappy scrapings.

Down by the seaside,
We await the eventide
That sweeps ashore our baiting,
At the idyllic country siding.

## *Shoddy Fatherhood*

Carelessly strewn
Wild oats,
Secretly sown recklessly
Far afield in youthful haste.
Too late to recall
Germinated oats,
Carelessly strewn far afield.

Ripened flowers,
Bountiful harvest,
Offshoots of secret breeds.
Arduous quest for recognition,
Unearthing sown secret seeds,
Begotten offsprings,
Ripened and strewn far afield.

## *Whiskers*

Whiskers, what whiskers?
What whiskers if I may ask?
Fuzzy and descriptive of me;
Wiry hairs atop my lip,
Moustached lip of hermaphrodite trait,
Grown overnight to spite my face.

Haste to shave off every strand,
Bald each time for smooth disguise.
Don't we all partake in this
Every waking morning?

Whiskers, what whiskers?
What whiskers are you yapping about?

# *Epilogue*

Queer, mystifying and baffling pieces in places.
Have all your niggling questions answered,
Have a dialogue with the author,
Write through the publishers for a *tête-à-tête*;
All mails replied.
Wait for Volume Two.

Printed in the United Kingdom
by Lightning Source UK Ltd.
126947UK00001B/7-21/P